FAVORITE FOOTBALL TEAMS

INDIANAPOLIS COLTS

BY K. C. KELLEY

THE CHILD'S WORLD®

1980 Lookout Drive • Mankato, MN 56003-1705
800-599-READ • www.childsworld.com

ACKNOWLEDGMENTS

The Child's World®: Mary Berendes, Publishing Director
Shoreline Publishing Group, LLC: James Buckley, Jr., Production Director
The Design Lab: Kathleen Petelinsek, Design;
 Gregory Lindholm, Page Production

PHOTOS

Cover: Focus on Football
Interior: AP/Wide World: 9, 18, 25 (Wayne); Focus on Football: 5, 6, 10, 13, 17,
 21, 23; Stockexpert: 14

Published in the United States of America.

LIBRARY OF CONGRESS CATALOGING-IN-PUBLICATION DATA

Kelley, K. C.
   Indianapolis Colts / by K.C. Kelley.
       p. cm. — (Favorite football teams)
   Includes bibliographical references and index.
   ISBN 978-1-60253-320-2 (library bound : alk. paper)
   1. Indianapolis Colts (Football team)—History—Juvenile literature. 2. Baltimore
Colts (Football team)—History—Juvenile literature. I. Title. II. Series.
   GV956.I53K45 2009
   796.332'640977252—dc22   2009009070

TABLE OF CONTENTS

Go, Colts!

The history of the Colts is like a roller coaster. For a while, they were one of the best teams. Then they weren't very good for a long time. In recent years, they've been back at the top. They have also played in two different cities! Wherever they play these days, the Indianapolis Colts are one of the best football teams around. Let's meet the Colts!

Here come the Colts! Cheerleaders and fans cheer as the Colts run onto the field for a 2008 game.

Who Are the Indianapolis Colts?

The Indianapolis Colts play in the National Football League (NFL). They are one of 32 teams in the NFL. The NFL includes the National Football Conference (NFC) and the American Football Conference (AFC). The Colts play in the South Division of the AFC. The winner of the NFC plays the winner of the AFC in the **Super Bowl**. The Colts have been the NFL champions four times!

The Colts show off their great teamwork. They combine to tackle this New England Patriots player in a 2008 game.

Where They Came From

The Colts didn't always play in Indianapolis. They started in Baltimore in 1953. They were the league champions by 1958. In 1984, the team moved to Indianapolis. There was one problem. The owners hadn't told Baltimore they were moving! It was a bad surprise for Baltimore but good news for Indianapolis!

This was one of the most famous plays in NFL history. The Colts' Alan Ameche scored a touchdown in overtime to win the 1958 NFL Championship Game.

10

Who They Play

The Colts play 16 games each season. There are three other teams in the AFC South. They are the Houston Texans, the Jacksonville Jaguars, and the Tennessee Titans. Every year, the Colts play each of these teams twice. They also play other teams in the NFC and AFC.

When the Colts and Titans play, it's a matchup of two of the best teams in the AFC.

Where They Play

The Colts play their home games at Lucas Oil Stadium. They used to play in the RCA Dome. It was a big indoor stadium. Lucas Oil Stadium opened in 2008. This huge outdoor stadium quickly became a fan favorite. If the weather gets bad, a roof rolls out over the stadium. But in good weather, the fans enjoy football in the sunshine!

Fans wearing blue and white fill Lucas Oil Stadium and cheer for the Colts.

13

goalpost

end zone

red zone

sideline

midfield

hash mark

red zone

goalpost

end zone

FOOTBALL

10
20
30
40
50
40
30
20
10

10
20
30
40
50
40
30
20
10

FOOTBALL

The Football Field

An NFL field is 100 yards long. At each end is an **end zone** that is another 10 yards deep. Short white **hash marks** on the field mark off every yard. Longer lines mark every five yards. Numbers on the field help fans know where the players are. Goalposts stand at the back of each end zone. On some plays, a team can kick the football through the goalposts to earn points. During the game, each team stands along one sideline of the field. The field at Lucas Oil Stadium is made of **artificial**, or fake, grass. Most outdoor NFL stadiums have real grass.

During a game, the two teams stand on the sidelines. They usually stand near midfield, waiting for their turns to play. Coaches walk on the sidelines, too, along with cheerleaders and photographers.

Big Days!

The Colts have had many great moments in their long history. Here are three of the greatest:

1958: The Baltimore Colts beat the New York Giants to win the NFL Championship Game. That contest is still known as "The Greatest Game Ever Played."

1971: The Colts won their first Super Bowl. Kicker Jim O'Brien made a **field goal** with only 5 seconds left! Baltimore won 16–13 over the Dallas Cowboys.

2007: The Colts won Super Bowl XLI. They beat the Chicago Bears 29–17.

Peyton Manning holds the Super Bowl trophy in 2007. Coach Tony Dungy is on the left. The two men led the Colts to their first championship in Indianapolis.

Tough Days!

The Colts can't win all their games. Some games or seasons don't turn out well. The players keep trying to play their best, though! Here are some painful memories from Colts history:

1969: The Colts were supposed to win Super Bowl III easily. Everyone thought they were much better than the New York Jets. But the Jets won! It was one of football's biggest upsets ever.

1981-1982: The Colts won only two games in these two seasons—combined! They also tied one game.

1991: The Colts won only one game . . . and lost 15!

Eric Dickerson (29) was one of the best players of all time. But in 1991, he and the Colts had a tough time in this game against the Cleveland Browns.

Meet the Fans

Colts fans actually live in two cities. Some fans of the original Baltimore Colts still root for the blue-and-white, even though the team has moved. (Other Baltimore football fans root for the Ravens, who replaced the Colts in that city.) In Indiana, Colts fans love their team. The Colts have enjoyed great success since **quarterback** Peyton Manning joined the team. He has made them one of the NFL's best teams.

Wow, these guys really like the Colts. Great fans like this have enjoyed watching the Colts win a lot of games!

21

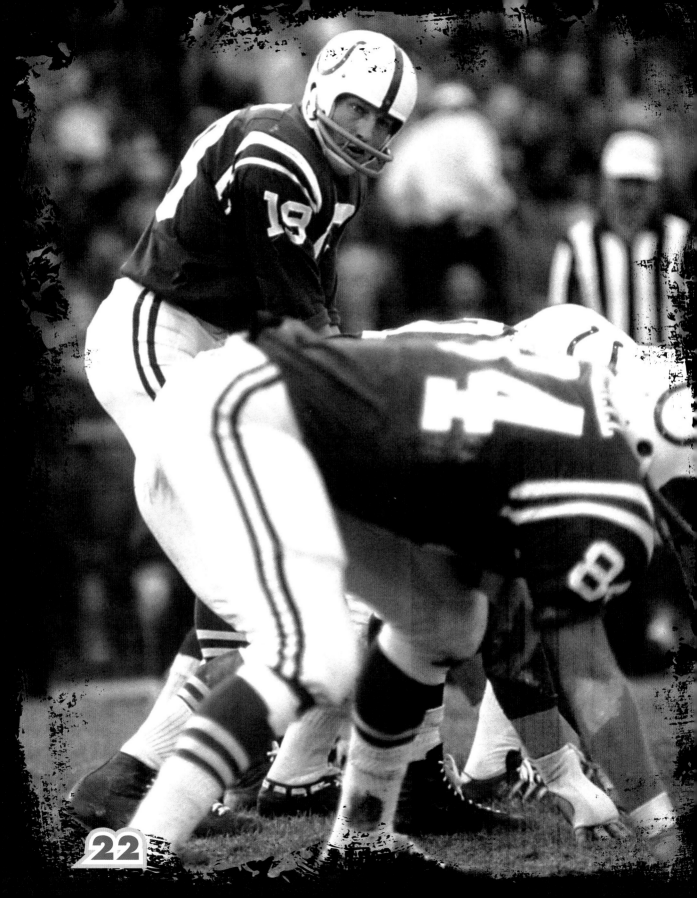

Heroes Then . . .

The greatest Colts players helped the team win NFL championships in 1958 and 1959. Some experts call Johnny Unitas the greatest quarterback ever. He was famous for moving his team quickly down the field. He set a record by throwing a touchdown pass in 47 games in a row! Many of those were caught by **receiver** Raymond Berry. He and Unitas worked together for hours. Berry caught just about anything thrown his way. **Running back** Lenny Moore was fast and talented. He scored touchdowns on runs and catches. On **defense**, Gino Marchetti tackled anyone carrying a football.

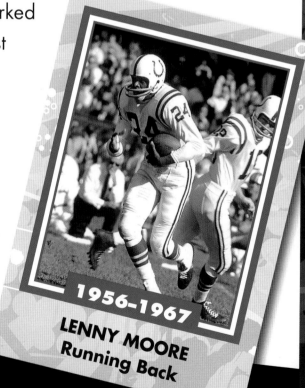

1956-1967

LENNY MOORE
Running Back

The great Johnny Unitas (left) was one of the best quarterbacks of all time. Here he stands at the line of scrimmage, ready to start the next play.

23

Heroes Now . . .

The Colts' biggest star is, of course, Peyton Manning. His great passing skills and leadership have made him a superstar. Peyton threw 49 touchdown passes in 2004. That was the most until New England's Tom Brady threw 50 in 2007. Peyton led the Colts **offense** to a Super Bowl win in the 2006 season. Speedy **wide receiver** Reggie Wayne has caught many of Peyton's passes. On defense, **safety** Bob Sanders is one of the NFL's toughest tacklers. **Defensive end** Dwight Freeney makes other quarterbacks tremble. He is among the best at making **sacks**.

PEYTON MANNING
Quarterback

REGGIE WAYNE
Wide Receiver

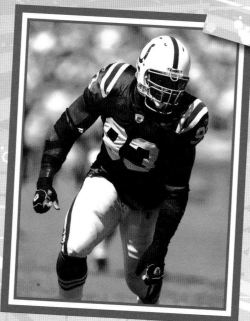

DWIGHT FREENEY
Defensive End

Gearing Up

Indianapolis Colts players wear lots of gear to help keep them safe. They wear pads from head to toe. Check out this picture of Peyton Manning and learn what NFL players wear.

The Football

NFL footballs are made of four pieces of leather. White laces help the quarterback grip and throw the ball. Inside the football is a rubber bag that holds air.

Football Fact

NFL footballs don't have white lines around them. Only college teams use footballs with those lines.

helmet

facemask

shoulder pad

chest pad

thigh pad

hand towel

knee pad

cleats

27

Sports Stats

Note: All numbers are through the 2008 season.

Touchdowns

TOUCHDOWN MAKERS

These players have scored the most touchdowns for the Colts.

PLAYER	TOUCHDOWNS
Marvin Harrison	128
Lenny Moore	113

PASSING FANCY

Top Colts quarterbacks

PLAYER	PASSING YARDS
Peyton Manning	45,628
Johnny Unitas	39,768

Quarterbacks

RUN FOR GLORY

Top Colts running backs

PLAYER	RUSHING YARDS
Edgerrin James	9,226
Lydell Mitchell	5,487

Running backs

Receivers

CATCH A STAR
Top Colts receivers

PLAYER	CATCHES
Marvin Harrison	1,102
Raymond Berry	631

TOP DEFENDERS
Colts defensive records

Most **interceptions**: Bobby Boyd, 57
Most sacks: Dwight Freeney, 70.5

Defenders

COACH
Most Coaching Wins

Tony Dungy, 92

Coach

29

Glossary

artificial fake, not real

defense players who are trying to keep the other team from scoring

defensive end a player who tries to tackle the other team's quarterback and running backs

end zone a 10-yard-deep area at each end of the field

field goal a three-point score made by kicking the ball between the upper goalposts

hash marks short white lines that mark off each yard on the football field

interceptions catches made by defensive players

line of scrimmage the place where the two teams face off when a play starts

offense players who have the ball and are trying to score

quarterback the key offensive player who starts each play and passes or hands off to a teammate

receiver an offensive player who catches forward passes

running back an offensive player who runs with the football and catches passes

sacks tackles of a quarterback behind the line of scrimmage

safety a defensive player who lines up farthest from the football and keeps receivers from making catches

Super Bowl the NFL's yearly championship game

touchdown a six-point score made by carrying or catching the ball in the end zone

wide receiver an offensive player who starts each play to one side of the team and runs to catch the ball

Find Out More

BOOKS

Buckley, James Jr. *The Scholastic Ultimate Book of Football*. New York: Scholastic, 2009.

Doeden, Matt. *Peyton Manning*. Minneapolis: Twenty-First Century Books, 2008.

Madden, John, and Bill Gutman. *Heroes of Football*. New York: Dutton, 2006.

Polzer, Tim. *Play Football! A Guide for Young Players from the National Football League*. New York: DK Publishing, 2002.

Stewart, Mark. *The Indianapolis Colts*. Chicago: Norwood House Press, 2006.

WEB SITE

Visit our Web site for lots of links about the Indianapolis Colts and other NFL football teams:

childsworld.com/links

Note to Parents, Teachers, and Librarians: We routinely verify our Web links to make sure they are safe, active sites—so encourage your readers to check them out!

Index

About the Author

K. C. Kelley is a huge football fan! He has written dozens of books on football and other sports for young readers. K. C. used to work for NFL Publishing and has covered several Super Bowls.